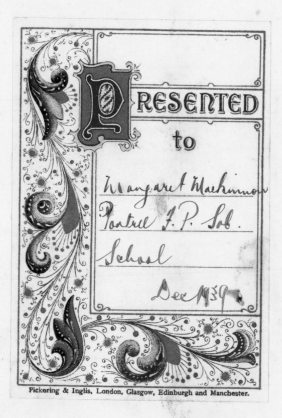

PRESENTED

to

Margaret Mackinnon
Poatrel F. P. Sab.
School

Dec 1939

Pickering & Inglis, London, Glasgow, Edinburgh and Manchester.

FLORENCE NIGHTINGALE   GRACE DARLING
MRS. JUDSON   MARY SLESSOR

TWELVE
WONDERFUL WOMEN

THE ROMANCE OF THEIR
LIFE AND WORK

BY

E. H. FARRANCE
Author of "Pepita, the Sea Lover," etc.

LONDON:
PICKERING & INGLIS Ltd.
14 PATERNOSTER ROW, E.C.4
Glasgow, Edinburgh, Manchester, Liverpool

LONDON -   - 14 PATERNOSTER ROW, E.C.4
GLASGOW -   - 229 BOTHWELL STREET, C.2
MANCHESTER - 135 DEANSGATE, 3
LIVERPOOL   - 5 HOPE WAY, 8
EDINBURGH   - 29 GEORGE IV BRIDGE, 1
NEW YORK   - LOIZEAUX BROS., 19 WEST 21ST ST.
TORONTO -   - HOME EVANGEL, 418 CHURCH ST., 2

TWELVE NOBLE LIVES

Titles as follows

Made and Printed in Great Britain   210385

Contents

Illustrations

TWELVE
WONDERFUL WOMEN

CHAPTER I

Florence Nightingale

IN March, 1854, war was declared with
Russia, and with "characteristic force
and devotion" Florence Nightingale
answered (as she believed) the "Call of God
to go forth to the Crimea to help." With
a selected company of thirty-eight ladies,
accompanied by Mr. and Mrs. Bracebridge,
a clergyman and a courier, Florence Nightingale, on October 21st, started from
London, and the devoted band arrived
at Scutari on November 5th.

FLORENCE NIGHTINGALE, the second
daughter of a wealthy English gentleman,
was born in Italy, in 1820. She spent the
summer months with her parents at their

home, "Lea Hurst," in Derbyshire; and as a girl she would often be seen in the village visiting the poor. She was well educated and a clever musician.

Florence Nightingale wished to use her strength, time, and money in service for the Lord Jesus Christ, and her great desire was to be a nurse. So when presented at Court she did not enter into the pleasures and scenes of gaiety; all her thoughts were centred upon her object, and she was full of ideas of providing better nursing for the sick poor. In those days Hospital nursing was looked upon with disfavour, and was not considered respectable. But these opinions had no weight with her; she threw her whole being into her project, and never missed an opportunity of visiting Hospitals in London, Dublin, Edinburgh, and abroad.

Upon their arrival at Scutari they found the hospital destitute of every comfort, the food supplies inadequate and unfit for use. But this loving and capable woman set herself to remedy these evils, and in ten days she had a proper kitchen fitted up and a laundry established. All this was done in the teeth of opposition, both active and passive, from those who afterwards learned to appreciate her and the changes she made, and became her true friends.

She was a brave woman. One who witnessed her work said: "She has frequently been known to stand for hours on the arrival of fresh detachments of sick, apportioning quarters, distributing stores, directing the operations where her presence might soothe or support, and she spent hours with men dying of cholera or fever."

Slowly, but surely, Miss Nightingale's influence made itself felt throughout the entire hospital. How she was appreciated by the soldiers! "To see her pass is happiness. She would speak to one, and nod and smile to many more, but she could not do it to all, you know. We lay there by hundreds; but we could kiss her shadow as it fell, and lay our heads upon the pillow again content. "

She would go her solitary rounds, a slight figure with a lamp shading it with her hand, lest its brightness should disturb the sleepers. Her energy and tact had brought order out of chaos, and practical efficiency out of hopeless failure.

The name of Florence Nightingale rang through the length and breadth of England. She had become, indeed, the "Heroine of the Crimea," and Queen Victoria sent a message to "Miss Florence Nightingale and to her devoted band of workers. "

But her tired "frame" was greatly worn by fatigue. She was a delicate woman, and the work at Scutari had tried her to the uttermost; she became ill with the Crimean fever, and for a fortnight she lay in great danger, and many earnest prayers went up for this unselfish woman. But with indomitable courage, when she recovered, instead of returning to England, she insisted on being at once taken back to her work at Scutari, and "with a heroism rarely equalled" she went back to nurse the sick there.

It will never be known how many dying soldiers were comforted and cheered, and how many (who knew not the Saviour) were led to Him in the eleventh hour by Florence Nightingale, and nothing was too small or apparently unimportant for her. She wrote letters home for the men who were unable to write; and when men died she generally took charge of their small bequests.

An old venerable pensioner at "The Chelsea Hospital" beside the Thames, once said:

"Many a time, when all was quiet at night, I've seen her coming through the wards with a little lamp in her hand, and every poor fellow who could not sleep was glad to see her. Ah! but when a man was dying, wasn't she good then! She'd sit with him, and read and talk. Oh! so

kindly, until it was all over.   God bless
her! That's what I say, sir."

Three months after Miss Nightingale's
return to Scutari the war with Russia was
brought to a close; and when Scutari
Hospital was closed, and the last soldier
returned home, the heroine of the Crimea's
work returned to England.

A tribute of praise was accorded her in
the House of Lords and also in the House
of Commons.   As a mark of National
gratitude it was suggested that "An
Institute for the training, sustenance, and
protection of Nurses and Hospital Atten-
dants should be started."

Gradually the work tended to concen-
trate itself around St. Thomas's Hospital,
where the Nightingale Home now stands,
and "from this Institution go forth year
by year a band of thoroughly trained
nurses, who in all parts of the world put
into practice the principles of 'nursing'
taught by Miss Nightingale, and so per-
petuate her priceless work."

For nearly forty years she was an invalid, confined to her couch; but the love of Christ constrained her, and gave her strength through ten years of conscientious preparation, through two years of unfaltering work in Scutari, and through all the subsequent years of suffering service. She not only gave her strength, time, and mind, but herself. She "passed away to be with Christ" at the honoured age of ninety, on August 13th, 1910.

CHAPTER II

Frances Ridley Havergal

MANY suns have risen and set since one December day in 1836, at Astley Rectory, in Worcestershire, FRANCES RIDLEY HAVERGAL was born. Her father, the Rev. William Havergal, and her mother (a beautiful woman), were earnest Christians. Her father had a decided musical gift—he composed many hymns and tunes; and doubtless Frances inherited his gift. The death of her mother, of whom she was very fond, when only eleven, nearly overwhelmed her with grief.

As a girl she was very anxious and longed to be a Christian—often would cry herself to sleep over her hopeless condition. But at last, through the earnest persuasion of two of her schoolfellows and the loving counsel of her step-mother, she trustfully yielded herself to her Saviour.

At eighteen she commenced her literary efforts.   Her first accepted contribution was her well-known hymn, "I Gave My Life for Thee."

It was suggested to her during a visit to Germany in 1858, through casually sitting down to rest opposite the picture of the Crucifixion which usually bore this motto. The verses flashed upon her like an inspiration, and she at once noted them down on a scrap of paper.   But she was not pleased with the result, and tossed them into the fire. As, however, the paper fell out unharmed, she decided to keep it. Some time after she showed them to her father, who was so favourably impressed that he wrote the tune "Baca" specially to go with them.

Then came a bitter disappointment, the pen was laid aside for nine years.   The outcome of this time of enforced rest of "coming apart for awhile," was her first

published book, "The Ministry of Song,"
which has inspired and comforted so many.

Frances was a wonderfully gifted
musician and an exquisite pianist. A
pupil of Beethoven once pronounced her
rendering of the Moonlight Sonata "per-
fect," and she would play through Handel,
much of Beethoven and Mendelssohn,
without any notes. When Frances went
on a visit to her married sister, Ellen, in
Ireland, she made a great impression with
her beautiful voice. It was one of her rich
gifts, and she had some very definite
thoughts about its use, *only* for God's
glory. She believed that "singing for
Jesus" was a most personal and direct
commission held for her Master.

Although outwardly brimful of life and
spirits, she never possessed really good
health. She had frequent breakdowns in
health and enforced rest. She had a wonderful belief in God's will for her, accepting
everything in a spirit of meek submission.
It was her custom to pray in private three

FRANCES RIDLEY HAVERGAL   HARRIET BEECHER STOWE
AGNES WESTON   PANDITA RAMABAI

To face page 16

FLORENCE NIGHTINGALE (KNOWN AS "THE LADY WITH THE
LAMP") GOING THROUGH THE HOSPITAL WARDS (Page 11)

times a day. She kept a paper in her Bible
with the subject of each prayer hour carefully arranged.

Her father died in 1870, and soon after
Frances began preparing Havergal's Psal-
mody for the press. Frances accepted the
thoughts and ideas that came to her as
sent direct from God—both in her musical
and poetic composition. She told a friend
once that she asked that at every line He
would give her not merely thoughts and
power, but also every word, even the very
rhymes. And very often, she said, she had
a most distinct and happy consciousness of
direct answers. It caused her deep joy to
hear that the poems or music were being
used and blessed by God, and she fully
realised the high privilege that was hers.
She wrote much: "The Ministry of Song,"
her first volume of poetry, published in
1869. "Under the Surface" and "Under
His Shadow" are beautiful heart experi-
ences and inspirations. These books have
been wonderfully blessed, they have

2

reached a circulation of hundreds of thousands. Her prose works are sweet and uplifting. "Kept for the Master's Use," "My King," "Royal Commandments," "Royal Bounty," etc. And her children's books are favourites: "Little Pillows," being good night thoughts for the little ones, and "Morning Bells," being waking thoughts for the little ones, and many others. Then hymns, sacred songs, and innumerable articles for magazines, booklets, and papers came from her pen. In her private correspondence, in her letters, her intense earnestness and loving reality were very markedly brought out. Her correspondence was voluminous, on all possible subjects. Of course, appeals for spiritual advice were always answered personally and at full length.

Frances Ridley Havergal was blessed in many ways. She travelled much, and kept a diary of these travels, with graphic descriptions of the scenery visited. During these journeys, wherever she went and

wherever she stopped, at every opportunity, she spoke of her Saviour. Her
whole personality proclaimed her happiness and the joy she possessed in the knowledge of her Lord and Saviour's love.
She was ever willing to give not only little
books and papers, but her own time and
energy—*herself*—to any who needed her
help.

The story of the writing of:

> "Take my life and let it be,
> Consecrated, Lord, to Thee"

is very interesting. Frances went to a
friend's house on a little visit of five days.
There were ten persons in the house, some
unconverted and long prayed for; some
converted, but not rejoicing Christians.
She prayed: "Lord, give me all this house,"
and her prayer was answered. Before she
left the house every one had got a blessing.

The last night of her visit she was too
happy to sleep, and she passed most of the
night in praise and renewal of her own
consecration; and then the little couplets

formed themselves and chimed in her heart one after another till they finished with: "Ever, only, all for Thee."

To her own nephews and nieces she was indeed a guiding, guardian angel. With all her many gifts, Frances was also an accomplished needle-woman; her work was exquisite, from darning to the most delicate lace work and embroidery. She had some decided opinions upon dress. Dress as a lady and as a Christian, unremarkably, yet with a general pleasing effect, then no attention is distracted; and she did not consider it right to spend on dress that which might be spared for God's work. And, too, her tongue and pen were ever eloquent on the theme of temperance. It was uppermost in her mind during the last weeks of her life.

On May 26th, 1879, she used her pen for the last time. On June 3rd, after acute suffering, following a chill, Frances Ridley Havergal "passed away to be with Christ," Whom she so faithfully loved and served.

This loving, gifted woman speaks to us
even to-day in her inspiring works, and
in her hymns, which are sung world wide.
How many have been thrilled and cheered
by the verse beginning:

"Lord Jesus, make Thyself to me,
A living, bright reality."

CHAPTER III

Agnes Weston the Sailors' Friend

AGNES WESTON was specially fitted for her noble life work, and she said: "God's hand has been on the tiller." Her parents were earnest Christians. Bath was the scene of her childhood and girl-hood.

When about seventeen, to quote her own words: "I saw myself as God saw me, as a sinner indeed, only to be saved by the Blood of Jesus Christ, God's Son . . . and as I rested my all upon the Saviour, the burden of sin rolled away, and I realised the glorious truth that He had borne my sins, and that by His stripes I was healed."

The years passed happily in work for the Master in various ways, and step by step God led her along into her life-work in the great Naval Service of the country.

Later on came the meeting with Miss
Wintz; and the forming of links in that
marvellous friendship which lasted un-
brokenly for so many years. They both
thought that they were capable of definite
work for God; and that they were drawn
together for a special purpose—and God
has in a wonderful way blessed their
united efforts for His glory.

In 1873, when Agnes Weston first went
to Devonport, four old ships were used as
training ships for the Royal Navy. She
began with boys; and the first meetings
they had were held in Mrs. Wintz's large
kitchen every Sunday afternoon. The
boys came cramming into the kitchen,
sitting on the floor and window sills when
the benches were full, and some on the
kitchen stove, with its cold plates. How
the boys sang! They read the Bible together and talked about it.

One of her earnest helpers was a curly
haired lad about seventeen. He was a
typical blue-jacket, bright and sunny,

and an earnest Christian. "I'll help you,"
he said to Miss Weston. "I'll go out into
the park and streets and fetch them in;
I'll be your recruiting sergeant." True to
his word, he would fetch them in, and
would come up the garden walk with a
dozen or so boys following him, and when
the room was full he was satisfied.

One day he said to her: "I'm sorry, but
I'm drafted to sea. I'm going this week to
the 'Triumph.' I shall miss those happy
Sunday afternoons." Miss Weston re-
minded him of the presence of Christ everywhere with us. "Yes," he said, "that's
true; it's my only comfort. He will help
me to stand up for Him and not to be
ashamed of my colours." They had some
prayer together, and he went away, saying:
"'The Triumph' will be here again in six
months, and when she drops her anchor in
Plymouth Sound I shall be up to the meeting like a shot."

Three months after the ship left, Miss
Weston had a letter from his captain. He

said: "We have had one of your boys on board, Arthur Phillips; he was a splendid seaman, and just been rated, and the Commander said one of the best royal yardsmen he ever had. His influence on board was remarkable; the men would stop swearing when he was near, because they said it hurt him so. He was never ashamed to kneel down under his hammock for prayer before the hands turned in. He had gone on the orlop deck during dinner for reading and for prayer as usual; one of the chain lockers had accidentally been left open, and in the darkness he had stepped into it and death was instantaneous."

Arthur Phillips's prayer was answered (prayed months before). The prayer was something like this: "O Lord, help to bring the boys up, and do them good when they come, and grant that this kitchen may be crowded out, and *that we may have to get another room,* for Jesus Christ's sake. Amen." And the first Sailors' Rest at Devonport was the outcome of this boy's prayer.

The work, whether at Devonport or Portsmouth, consists of two departments; both being linked together. The Hall, with its evangelistic work, Bible classes, gatherings for sailors' wives and children, temperance and other social meetings. And the Institute, with its refreshment bar, dormitories, baths, dining and reading rooms. When the men come home, they make for the Sailors' Rest, and they always find something to help them. They have meetings for the study of the Bible and for prayer; and a quiet room in each of the Sailors' Rests where men so minded can talk and pray.

Miss Weston always had a band of excellent workers, men who had been in the service and knew all about it; they were always about the Sailors' Rest, ready to chat with men, to read or pray with them, and to help in every way. These Rests have over 1400 beds between them.

The Royal Naval Temperance Society, the uphill work of so many years, and the

Royal Naval Christian Union, numbering some 25,000 members scattered all over the world, have their headquarters at the Royal Sailors' Rests.

In the year 1887, Jubilee year, they had a visit from the Crown Princess of Germany, our Princess Royal. She was delighted with the place, which she inspected minutely. As Miss Weston guided her through the reading rooms, she noticed the presence of a Bible on each table, among all the magazines and periodicals. Turning to Miss Weston, she said: "I am so glad to see the Bible, the best Book of all, among the papers, and I can also see it has been well read."

Miss Weston told Her Royal Highness what she felt about the Bible. "Yes," she replied, "it is the crown of your work."

The Sailors' Rests not only contain sleeping accommodation, but restaurants (open to the public), brilliant with electric light, mirrors, silver urns, and marble-topped tables. No gambling—no one

turned away.   What a blessing; what a
boon for the blue-jackets to look forward
to when far away from home, on the lonely
wide ocean.   These Rests are of great good
to the State.

Every Sunday evening the halls at
Devonport and Portsmouth are crowded
by seafaring men, soldiers, and marines,
sailors' wives and mothers, pensioners
from the service, etc.   At their meetings
many decisions are made, and many a
heart and life are surrendered to God.
A Christian in the Navy is greatly per-
secuted, it is no "lavender water life."
They are made fun of, yet their persecutors
know that they can be trusted.

The late Queen Victoria took a great
deal of interest in these Rests, and in
response to Her Majesty's desire to hear
about the work, Miss Weston went to
Windsor.

She did much for the sailors' wives
(many of them are earnest Christians)
during the absence of their husbands on

the sea; also for the boys and girls.   Her
monthly letters, "Ashore and Afloat,"
sent out to her blue-jackets, have been a
power for good.

Toward the close of her life she said:
"I realise every day, more and more, that
it is only as God works through us that we
can do anything.   The failures and mis-
takes have been mine, and the glory is
God's."

The Sailors' Rests are wonderful wit-
nesses to the faithfulness of God.

CHAPTER IV

Fanny Jane Crosby

"NOTHING of education, or culture, or breeding, can take the place of Christ in the home—of Jesus in the heart." These are the words of FANNY JANE CROSBY, born in the year 1820, in the South-East Putnam County, New York. She came from a devout and hardy race—the Crosby's, descendants of William Brewster, one of the noble band of Pilgrim Fathers.

She was blind from six weeks old, and her mother, grandmother, and a dear old Quaker friend were among her first instructors. She was eager for an education, and although loving her home and mother, was ready and willing to go away in order to be educated.

When she was told she was going to
enter the Institution for the Blind in New
York City, she clapped her hands and
said: "Thank God! He has answered my
prayer." As pupil and teacher she remained in the Institution for twenty years.

Fanny Crosby was converted on November 20th, 1850, at a revival meeting held
in the Thirteenth Street Methodist Church.
She had been anxious for some time, and
that evening the congregation was singing
the hymn:

> "Alas! and did my Saviour bleed,
>   And did my Sovereign die?"

When they reached the line of the fourth
stanza:

> "Here Lord I give myself away"

she said: "My very soul was flooded with
celestial light. I sprang to my feet,
shouting 'Hallelujah!' and then, for the
first time I realised that I had been trying
to hold the world in one hand and the
Lord in the other."

Fanny Crosby was taken to Congress

in 1843, and she recited a number of her poems, which were well received. Then awoke a deep longing for literature and friendship. She was greatly interested in all the U.S. Presidents, but Abraham Lincoln was her "Captain, her leader." It was with Grover Cleveland that she was brought into closer touch than with any of the other Presidents. He was Secretary to the Institution for the Blind, and she often went to him with her heartaches, and he always proved a sympathetic friend. He copied for her many of her poems, and he took an interest in her life and work. During the years at the Institution, Fanny Crosby heard the best music, and read the purest in poetry and prose.

From her eighth year she wrote little poetic pictures. She said: "When I gathered flowers, and caught their fragrance I wanted to say something poetic about them. When I heard the birds sing I was anxious to understand their notes. As I wandered down by the brook with my

By courtesy of Indian Railways Bureau

A TYPICAL BURMESE GIRL
(Chapter V)

PUPILS OF PANDITA RAMABAI AT THE SHARADA SADAN, POONA (Chapter VI)

grandmother listening to the rippling of
the waters, I felt something in my soul
that I wanted to say about the rivulet
and river. " She wrote poems for special
occasions, and in 1844 she published her
book: "The Blind Girl, and Other Poems. "
She met with many noted people when
they visited the Blind Institution.

At thirty-eight, Fanny Crosby married
Van Alstyne, a gifted blind student who
came to the Institution. He was a firm
trusting Christian, and they were happy
together for over forty years.

Fanny Crosby had written a large number
of secular and religious poems, a few
cantatas and many songs; but her real
writing of Christian hymns began when
she left the Institution and became associated with some notable religious leaders.
A friend one day played over a tune and
she exclaimed: "That says, 'Safe in the
Arms of Jesus,' " and went into her room
and in about thirty minutes returned with
the hymn: "Safe in the Arms of Jesus, "

3

and she was told that *that* hymn gave great comfort to mothers who had lost their children.

Altogether her hymns and poems total eight thousand. One of her hymns that won world-wide attention was: "Pass me not, O gentle Saviour," written in the year 1868. Mr. Sankey said: "No hymn in our collection was more popular than this one at the meetings in London in 1874." This hymn has been translated into many foreign languages. Also: "Rescue the Perishing," "Saved by Grace," and "Blessed Assurance;" and others, have been the means of wonderful blessing to many a one.

In conversation with a friend one day, Fanny Crosby said, as she took a little New Testament from her bag: "When I was a child, this Book had a practical place in the home and the nation. During these many years my love for the Holy Bible has not waned. Its truth was not only born with me, it was bred into my life. My mother and my grandmother took pains that I knew the Bible better than any other book. All that I am, and all that I ever expect to be in literature or life, is due to the Bible."

And at ninety years of age, she said: "My love for the Holy Bible and its sacred truth is stronger and more precious to me at ninety than at nineteen. This Book to me is 'God's Treasure-house,' and there is nothing I love better than to have my friends read to me from the sacred page."

Fanny Crosby was a loving, sympathetic woman, ever ready to minister to those in sorrow, and to give pleasure by her birthday poems to her friends. Joyousness was one of the characteristics of her life.

At the age of ninety-two, Fanny Crosby visited Harvard College, and for a brief space came under the influence of literary and educational power. She conversed with the Professors, and she told them that one of her ancestors, Simon Crosby, was one of its founders, and that his son

graduated therefrom in 1653. She said it
was a joy to associate with such men.
She said: "In sunshine or shadow, in sickness, in health, through every step of the
journey God has given grace and glory.
There is nothing surprising in this. It is
according to the promise. And no good
thing will He withhold from them that
walk uprightly! It is the things I have
had in full measure in which I rejoice
daily."

At ninety years of age she said: "I am
living in the sight of Eternity's sunrise. . .
I have made a careful study of human
nature, I know a person by the touch of
the hand, or the sound of the voice. Even
the footstep is to me a token of the char-
acter of its owner. I have been careful of
cultivating a sunny disposition, for I have
found in my experience so many who,
when they grow old, become difficult to
get along with. My simple trust in God's
goodness has never failed me during these
many years. There is nothing in this wide

world that gives me so much joy as telling
the story of my Saviour's loving mercy."

In a verse of her beautiful hymn, "Saved
by Grace," she wrote:

> "Some day the silver cord will break,
>   And I no more, as now, shall sing.
> But, oh! the joy when I shall wake,
>   Within the palace of the King!
> And I shall see Him face to face,
>   And tell the story—saved by grace."

The "silver cord broke" on February
12th, 1915, and this sweet hymn writer
and singer "passed away to be with Christ."
She was rich in faith, hope, and love, and
her hymns will ever live.

CHAPTER V

Ann H. Judson

ANN HASSELTINE of Bradford (America) was betrothed to ADONIRAM JUDSON. He was about to sail for the foreign mission field. He placed before her all the hardships, loneliness, and dangers which a missionary's wife might be exposed to. But she prayerfully and carefully considered the matter, and with great heroism, for thus far no woman had ever left America as a missionary, and many friends opposed the undertaking as wild and visionary, made the decision and yielded herself to God for His work. They were married in February, 1812, and sailed together for the foreign mission field.

Burma was the goal of their desire. Mrs. Judson wrote: "that it presented a very extensive field for usefulness, con-

taining 17,000 inhabitants, and that the
Scriptures had never been translated into
their language. " India was then ruled by
the East India Company, which was
bitterly opposed to the introduction of
Christianity among the natives. The
Company professed to believe that the
natives would be offended by the introduction of a new religion.

Many attempts had already been made
to evangelise Burma, but the missionaries
died or left the Station, and only Felix
Carey (son of the famous Dr. Carey) and
his wife were left at Rangoon.

On their landing, after being searched
at the Custom house, they arrived at Mrs.
Carey's home—the house built of teak,
large and convenient, half a mile from the
town, with two acres of ground full of
fruit trees. In this spot they found a home,
where they could labour for the Saviour.

The Government of Burma when Mr.
and Mrs. Judson arrived was an absolute
despotism. The king had supreme power

over the life and possession of every subject. He could confiscate property, improvise torture, or execute at his pleasure—his only restraint being fear of insurrection.

Mr. and Mrs. Judson commenced to learn the language, but found many difficulties, as their teacher could not speak English. Their progress was slow, but they zealously pursued their studies, longing for the time when they could proclaim to the Burmese the glorious Gospel.

After three years of hard work at the language, Mr. and Mrs. Judson were then able to converse. Mr. Judson prepared a grammar, two tracts, and was working on a translation of Matthew's Gospel. So they were greatly delighted when in October, 1816, Mr. and Mrs. Hough arrived, bringing with them a printing press with Burman type from the American Baptist Society. Mrs. Judson commenced a meeting for women, which was held every Lord's Day. She prayed with them and taught them the Scriptures.

Thrilling indeed are the adventures these two brave pioneers were called upon to go through. Cholera was raging in the town, and rumours of war with Britain caused the English ships to leave the port, inducing the Houghs to leave, but others came and the Mission began to grow.

In 1818 the Zayat was opened. It was a building in which to hold public worship on Sundays in Burman. On the Lord's Day, May 9th, they had a great joy— Moung Nan confessed Christ and later was baptised, proving a valuable assistant to Mr. Judson, and was eager to win others for Christ. They had long been sowing, and now their reaping time had come. It must indeed have been a cheer to their loving hearts to see one and another come out for the Truth.

It is most interesting to follow how God's work slowly prospered in spite of hindrances. November 10th was a special red letter day. The first Burman Prayer Meeting that was ever held—only Mr.

Judson was present and the three converts. On the following day—the Lord's Day—those three converts met at the Zayat, and held a prayer meeting of their own accord.

But a dark cloud was gathering. War was impending between Burma and England, and for two years news of them was cut off from the Christians in America. They were in great suspense. The occasion of the war was Chittagong, which was under British protectorate and which the Burmese Emperor desired to possess. With this design, the Emperor collected an army of 30,000 men; but the Bengal Government anticipating the blow, sent in May, 1821, an army who attacked and captured Rangoon; and after a series of engagements, penetrated to Yandaboo, about forty miles from the capital.

While the British were advancing the missionaries were passing through a time of awful tribulation. They were being tested to the uttermost. For several weeks nothing took place, and they went on with their work as usual.

A rumour was afloat that the Englishmen were spies, and Mr. Judson was arrested and bound brutally with tight cords and dragged off, and later Dr. Price. In vain Mrs. Judson offered money for his cords to be loosed, but they threw Mr. Judson on the ground and drew the cords still tighter. The officer and his gang proceeded to the court-house; an order was read, and Mr. Judson was hurled into the death prison and the door closed. It was a time of keen anguish for Mrs. Judson, but she found solace in prayer. Then this brave woman spared no pains in trying to get their release, but to no purpose. She obtained permission to visit the governor of the city, and after presenting a handsome gift, she was given an order to visit the prison. But when she saw Mr. Judson, who crawled to the door of the prison, it was almost too much for her. The interview was sad and tense.

Mrs. Judson also made a petition to the Queen, but it failed, and her hopes were dashed to the ground. Then she was permitted to make a little bamboo room in the prison enclosure, where Mr. Judson could be much by himself, and she was sometimes allowed to spend two or three hours. In the midst of all these tribulations a little daughter was born, and she was unable to visit. The poor prisoners were suffering intensely through the heat and loss of appetite.

Mrs. Judson made daily application to the governor, offering him money, which he refused. Then Mrs. Judson was taken with a fever. Later the prisoners were removed without her knowledge, and after a painful search (with her three months' old baby), she found them at Oung-peu-la. The brutal treatment they received was astounding. They were tied two and two and driven along like slaves for eight miles on a hot road of sand and gravel. While Mrs. Judson was at Oung-peu-la, she was

taken very ill, and consequently her little
baby, Maria, suffered, too. It seemed as
if her cup was now full, but in the midst
of all these great calamities her faith never
failed, and she had an "assured conviction
that every additional trial was ordered by
infinite love and mercy."

But it was God's will that husband and
wife should be separated again. Mr.
Judson was sent to the Burman Camp to
act as translator and interpreter. Mrs.
Judson was seized with spotted fever,
with all its attendant horrors. The day
she was taken ill with fever a Burmese
nurse came and offered her help for Maria.
The circumstance filled her with gratitude
and confidence in God. God did indeed
answer their prayers. They were released,
and reached the Mission Camp at Rangoon
after an absence of two years and three
months.

The treaty of peace between the British
and the Burmese was signed on February
24th, 1826. Mr. and Mrs. Judson, now in

Rangoon, turned to their life-work with ardour, for Mr. Judson had rapidly recovered from the effects of his imprisonment. They thought well to remove the Mission to a place under the protection of British Government, and arrangements were made to settle at Amherst. Before settling, Mr. Judson went to Ava on business. He was away about two and a half months, and while away he received the news of his beloved wife's death. After his departure Mrs. Judson had built a little bamboo dwelling-house and two school-houses. In one of these she gathered ten Burman children, who were placed under Moung Ing, whilst she herself assembled the few native converts for worship every Sunday.

But in the midst of her labours she was smitten with fever, and "passed away to be with Christ" on October 24th, 1826, in her thirty-seventh year. She loyally served the Lord, and was one of the bravest missionary women who ever lived.

CHAPTER VI

Pandita Ramabai

THE "Friend of India's child-widows" was born in April, 1858. Her father had advanced views on female education, and Ramabai at an early age acquired many dialects, taught by her fond mother, and at the age of twelve had committed to memory no less than 1800 verses from the Scriptures of Hinduism.

Great were the hardships that Ramabai and her sister and brother suffered with their parents, and when they were left orphans, and only Ramabai and her brother remained, the two travelled on foot, the brother sometimes getting work to do at wretchedly low wages. Two results—the outcoming of these trampings—were that the brother and sister gradually lost faith in the Hindu religion and gained, through

what they saw and heard, increased en-
thusiasm in the cause of the down-trodden
Hindu women. They gained the public
ear—and then their days of poverty and
privation were over.

Ramabai's learning was astounding—
she was mistress of seven languages, as
well as of the sacred books. Together
Ramabai and her brother travelled
throughout Bengal, holding meetings on
the education and emancipation of
women. But the privations and hardships had undermined the brother's
strength, and he died—then Ramabai was
left alone.

At twenty-two years of age Ramabai
married a Bengali gentleman, a graduate
of Calcutta University, Bipin Bihari
Medhani, M.A. When their little daughter
Manorama was twelve months old,
Ramabai's husband died.

Ramabai's emancipation and education gave her a tremendous advantage,
and after her husband's death, bravely

rising above her own grief, she set herself to alleviate the misery and bitter sorrow of the child-widows.

The sufferings of the child-widow whose husband has died before the culmination of their marriage are lamentable. It is considered a sure sign that the poor little girl in a previous state committed some fearful crime—such is the darkness and superstition. She has to work hard, suffer the most brutal blows; she is not allowed to join any family gathering, or in any festivity. And this treatment is in the home of her mother-in-law, as long as her life lasts. Poor little thing! This, then, was the class to which Ramabai herself now belonged, and whose champion she now became.

Ramabai's first protege was a poor little arab of the streets, a Brahmin child twelve years old, cast out by her husband's relations after his death. This little homeless wanderer Ramabai took under her protection, and she is now leading a happy

4

and useful life as a Christian Bible-woman.

But there were myriads of others. In 1891, the number of widows in India was estimated at 23,000,000, many of them quite young girls and children, in similarly wretched cases, and Ramabai could not rest till she had wrought some practical work for the alleviation of their lot.

All this time she was seeking for the *Truth*; she procured a Bible and began to study its teachings. After her husband's death, for a while she supported herself and her little daughter by lecturing on the education of women.

In 1882 she spoke before a British Commission on the question of education in India. She was well received. Soon after this Ramabai wanted to improve her education and acquaint herself with the English language and literature. She came with her little daughter to England, and stayed at an Anglican Sisterhood at Wantage. While there she "embraced the

Christian Faith," and with her little Manorama was baptised according to the rites of the Church of England.

After that she accepted the post of Professor of Sanskrit at the Cheltenham Ladies' College, which she held for a year and a half, continuing her own studies at the same time. Then she stayed in America three years, taking every opportunity of studying the educational methods of that country, and especially the kindergarten system, which greatly aroused her interest. She also travelled much, with a view to enlisting public sympathy in the important scheme which was now definitely shaping itself in her mind. This was to found a school where Hindu widows of high caste could be received and educated by their own countrywomen in such a way as to enable them to earn their own living when their school course was finished. Especially did Ramabai hope to train teachers who might be received into native homes, and even penetrate the seclusion of the Zenana itself with the light of knowledge and truth.

In 1887, in America, this Indian widow formed the "Ramabai Association," their headquarters were in Boston, the Presidents and Vice-Presidents including representatives of five religious denominations; the Board of Trustees secured some of the best business intellect of that city, and the Executive Committee was composed entirely of women. Its object was the formation of "circles" in every part of the States, which should pledge themselves to provide a certain sum annually for ten years, to start and maintain a home and school in India for high caste widows.

After travelling and speaking throughout Canada, and in most of the cities on the Pacific Coast, Ramabai set out for her Indian home, and landed in Bombay early in the year 1889, and in the spring opened her Widows' Home in the busy Anglo-Indian city of Bombay. Ramabai called her Home "Sharada Sadan," or, "Abode of Wisdom." She commenced with two pupils. The school increased rapidly, and was removed to Poona. This Home must have been a delightful place to the child-widow, the outcast, the hated one, standing in a garden with fine shady trees, gold mohur, and others; roses, lilies, jasmine, elemanta, and very many other beautiful plants, a fernery around a fountain. The pupils came and went everywhere, learned their lessons in the drawing-room, or walked in the garden and were allowed to gather the flowers. Ramabai was anxious for them to see the contrast where love ruled. No wonder they loved her. And although in Sharada Sadan every one was allowed to maintain her own religion, is it to be wondered at that the religion which was known to be the source of Ramabai's motherly love should attract and win over some of these young hearts.

It was the custom of Ramabai to meet with her companion-helper, Soonderbai,

and her little girl, Manorama, for Bible
reading and prayer every morning before
the duties of the day were begun. If any
of the pupils voluntarily chose to join
them, they, of course, were welcomed.
As time went on, quite half the widows
came to this family worship, several apparently being deeply impressed. But
this caused opposition, which Ramabai
and her American "weathered. "

To support her school, the idea came to
her to start a fruit farm. But her scheme
met with disappointment. Returning from
Bombay, she was very heavy-hearted; but
she encouraged herself in the Lord, and
she and her friend, Soonderbai Powar,
agreed to pray about it. Not long after
she was awakened very early one morning,
and a cablegram from America put into
her hand. She opened it—her faith was
honoured—*the farm was hers.*

The terrible famine of 1897 aroused the
ardent desire of Ramabai to do something
for the rescue of the hundreds of young

widows. Her faith was strong. Money flowed in, and she was enabled to help in a marvellous degree.

So at Khedgaon stand premises called "Mukti," which means "Salvation."

It was reported in 1899 to be in a flourishing condition, both as to its temporal and spiritual work. Many industries were carried on—dairy work, oil making, the cultivation of grain and red pepper, and the weaving of sarees upon hand-looms being among the most profitable. Her aim was to train the girls to do some kind of work. The colony now consists of eight hundred widows.

In the midst of all her cares and responsibilities, Ramabai trusted her loving Father, and was always sunny and young. Her great faith was the secret of the wonderful success of her noble life-work. She was called to her Rest on April 5, 1922, at the age of 64, but the work abides.

Fuller details in "PANDITA RAMABAI: Her Life and Work," by HELEN S. DYER. 4/ post free.

CHAPTER VII

Mrs. Walter Searle

MRS. SEARLE was born in 1846, in Birmingham. From her earliest childhood God was evidently preparing and fitting her for future service. As a child she was very unselfish, caring for the poor. She always said: "I do want to do a little thing for God to-day."

Her conversion, at the age of fourteen, she registered in her Bible—in the margin of the third chapter of Revelation: "These verses 15 and 16, preached from by dear Govett, of Norwich, led to my conversion in the Tivetshall Mission Hall, 1860." Govett was an evangelical preacher of the Church of England, and the Mission Hall referred to was built by her father, a godly squire.

From the first she sought to win others for Christ. She was married to Rev. Walter

Searle, on August 26th, 1875. They settled in Plymouth, and there commenced to work for the Lord. In 1879 they went to Birmingham, where her husband took the oversight of a new suburban Church. Here for thirteen years she laboured unceasingly, addressing various meetings: the Gospel, rescue work, temperance, ladies' Bible readings, mothers' meetings, and working men's Bible class, also using her "pen" in His service. But the home training of her children was not neglected.

Mrs. Searle nobly contended for the truth of the infallibility of the Scriptures. About a mile from Mr. Searle's Church (Westminster Road Church, Birmingham), there was a large ammunition factory, with about two thousand operatives, and some of them became members of her Bible Class for working men only, no one under twenty being allowed to join. One of these men, who, in despair had resolved to commit suicide, was led to attend, and like the jailer was suddenly and soundly

converted, and after spending many years
in earnest devotion to Christ, died tri-
umphantly.

The only attraction in her meeting was
the Cross—the blessed Word of the Living
God.   She firmly believed in the Bible.
She was greatly blessed in her Bible Class,
many, very many souls were won for Christ.

Mrs. Searle had a unique personality
with its attractive charm and skilful tact-
fulness; but all her work she achieved
through the power of the Holy Ghost.
She wrote: "We influence most by what
we are, not by what we do or say."

Mr. Searle was offered the post of
secretary to the S. Africa General Mission,
which grew up out of the life and labours
of Spencer Walton, and he accepted it.
Mrs. Searle decided to join the Mission
after wonderful clear guidance from the
Lord; and the whole family sailed from
Southampton, on November 5th, 1892.
Farewell meetings were held in Birmingham, and at Exeter Hall, London, when

Mrs. Searle gave her last message; explaining "how unerringly God had led her in obedience to the heavenly vision, to leave her native land for the Regions Beyond."

Just at this point I might quote from a letter I received a while ago from a dear Christian who is earnestly living for God's glory, and who daily seeks to yield her will to His will; "Mr. Searle was used of God when I was at Westminster Road Chapel to speak to me while I was in great distress of soul. He did not know it until the blow of losing my dear mother, which God used to break me down and bring me out to Himself. I look back and see how God's ways are wonderful. I had sweet fellowship with them for more than twenty years. Mrs. Searle was a woman of prayer, and so was her husband; you felt God's presence with them. I shall never forget the last time I saw them in London, just as they returned to South Africa for the last time. It was during the war, when travelling was so dangerous—how, as we all went before

God, they put me in God's hands and
themselves too, knowing the dangers before
them.   In faith they went.   How their
memory brings joy to my heart. "

They arrived at Cape Town, November
23rd, 1892.   Mrs. Searle's life at Cape
Town was a busy one, receiving visitors
at the Mission House, writing and speaking
filled her days.   But her special work,
which was greatly blessed, was her unde-
nominational Bible Class for ladies, held
in one of the loveliest suburbs.   Both felt
they heard God's call to "go forward, "
but they waited two years in Natal before
going onward, and there learnt further
lessons, serviceable and even essential,
for ministry among the natives.

So they went to Lutubeni, a lovely spot
once occupied by a trader's iron store for
natives, in the midst of a heathen district,
where the only dwellings are native mud
huts with thatched roofs, inhabited by the
raw red Kaffir.   The people are ignorant
and superstitious, terrorised by satanic

witch doctors, bound by vilest customs, addicted to daily drunkenness and accustomed to tribal feuds and fights which often end fatally. Here, then, was the glorious opportunity of naming Christ, where He was not known. They purchased the trader's store, and transformed it into school and church.

Lutubeni consisted of three mud huts, this was their first home among the heathen. Unfavourable, environment and unexpected difficulties did not daunt them. Mrs. Searle remembered Whittier's words: "We are not here to play, to dream, to drift. We have hard work to do and loads to lift. Shun not the struggle!" And the grace of God nerved her. They stayed there many years, and were privileged to witness a gracious outpouring of revival power. On a blank page in a little book, she wrote: "Great praise to God for giving me the desire to rise at six in the morning, to spend the first hour with Jesus my Saviour."

In Africa, in spite of climate, the hour was changed from six to five; the practice continued up to her last days. She has written in her Bible, at Psalm 87. 7, "All my springs are in Thee," and makes reference to David, her very own, by adding, "Yes, dear Lord, all." This was the secret of her service.

Turning to her last Scofield Bible, used from 1914 to her death, we read at the end of the first of Chronicles, this solemn declaration: "In this last chapter I am so truly thankful that I do offer my Lord all I am, and all I have, and I think it has been so for forty years and more."

Only Eternity will reveal the work she so faithfully did for her Lord and Master, whom she so dearly loved. She "fell asleep in Jesus" at Lutubeni, Tembuland, South Africa, on Monday evening, January 19th, 1925.

A full record of the remarkable work of Mrs. Searle is issued under the title, "She Loved Much," with illustrations. *Christian Herald* Office, or 14 Paternoster Row, E.C.4 2/6 net (2/10 post free). It is a stimulating book which should be read by all interested in Foreign Missions.

CHAPTER VIII

Harriet Beecher Stowe

WHO has not read "Uncle Tom's Cabin?" The book which has brought tears to the eyes of many a man and woman. Its circulation has been exceeded by that of no book, save the Bible and perhaps "Pilgrim's Progress," and it was "the wedge that finally rent asunder the gigantic fabric of American slavery with a fearful crash."

"Uncle Tom's Cabin" takes its place as a standard work amongst the beauties of English literature. It has been translated in France, Holland, Italy, Sweden, Russia, Spain, and other lands.

HARRIET BEECHER STOWE, the author of this wonderful book, was born on June

14, 1811, at Litchfield, Connecticut, where her father, Dr. Lyman Beecher, was an earnest pastor of a church. The mother was tender, gentle. and sympathising; she died when Harriet was quite young.

When Harriet was thirteen she "came to Jesus as she was, weary, and worn, and sad." As she said to her father: "I have given myself to Jesus, and He has taken me."

In 1832 her father accepted the presidency of the newly-established Lane Theological Seminary at Walnut Hills, near Connecticut, Ohio, and the whole family removed there. Cincinnati is a city situated on the northern bank of the Ohio; and upon the high hill, overhanging the City of the West, was Lane Seminary. The village nearest to it was called the Walnut Hills.

Harriet spent eighteen years in Lane Seminary. Her marriage with Professor E. Stowe, of Lane Seminary, over which her father was then President, proved very

ELIZABETH FRY   FANNY JANE CROSBY
MRS. WALTER SEARLE   CHARLOTTE MARIA TUCKER

To face page 64

A SLAVE GIRL BEING SOLD BY AUCTION IN THE DAYS OF
HARRIET BEECHER STOWE   (Page 67)

happy. She experienced a great sorrow when her much-loved little boy, Charlie, died of cholera. During that sorrow, Mrs Beecher Stowe prayed to God that such anguish might not be suffered in vain— and she desired "that the crushing of my own heart might enable me to work out some great good to others."

The road which ran through Walnut Hills, only a few feet from Mrs. Stowe's door, was a favourite route of "The Underground Railway," so-called. The railway consisted of a noble line of Quakers, and other anti-slavery friends, who lived at intervals of fifteen or twenty miles between the Ohio River and the Northern Lakes. These friends had combined to help fugitive slaves forward in their escape to Canada. A fugitive would be taken at night on horseback, or in a covered wagon, from station to station, until he stood on free soil. When a slave escaped to Canada, immediately his foot touched the soil he was free—his old master had no claim

5

upon him, and the days of his bondage were over, he was under a *new law*. This was given as an illustration at a meeting. The speaker was speaking about the law of the Spirit and the law of sin and death in Romans 8. 2. It was an apt illustration of the wonderful liberty of those who through faith are in Christ Jesus.

The first Station on the "Underground Railway" north of Cincinnati, was a few miles up Mill Creek, at the lonely farmhouse of a man named Van Sant. Mrs. Stowe would be frequently roused by the rapid rattle of the covered wagons and the noisy galloping of the horses, ridden by the constables and slave-catchers in hot pursuit, as they madly passed the door. Van Sant was always ready to turn out with his team, and the hunters were rarely clever enough to come up with them.

To more than one of these trembling fugitives Mrs. Stowe herself had given shelter, and wept bitter tears with them. She was touched with compassion for them, and ardently longed "to work out some great good" for their redress. She realised that the negro race were God's creatures, for whom Christ died. They were included in the message: "The Lord Jesus, who was made a little lower than the angels for the suffering of death, crowned with glory and honour; that *He* by the grace of God should taste death for *every man*" (Heb. 2. 9).

Mrs. Beecher Stowe decided to produce a book which would show the wickedness and horror of the slave-trade, and promote its overthrow.

A common sight which she visualised —crowd collected around a stand groups of negroes are huddled together, there is an examination of muscle, teeth, and the exhibition of agility. The negroes are frantic with terror at the idea of being sent down South, and the almost certainty that one member of a family will be torn from another; the anxious scanning of purchasers' faces, and the agony of parting (often for ever) with husband, wife, or child.   These poor slaves had no rights, they were wholly the property of their owners.   Such a scene may have been witnessed by Harriet when a girl, and filled her with a great compassion.

She wrote several tales and sketches for the magazine; but "Uncle Tom's Cabin" was her *masterpiece*. Nearly all her characters were taken from life.   Her *hero* was a slave, as she wrote, "born a slave, under a heathen—he grew up without Christian light or knowledge. One sermon, one offer of salvation by Christ, was sufficient for him to make him at once a believer from the heart and a preacher of Jesus."

No story was ever written that so deeply stirred the hearts and consciences of the English and American people.   "Uncle Tom's Cabin" was published in 1852. Ten thousand copies were sold in a few days and over three hundred thousand within a year; and eight power presses, running day and night, were barely able to keep pace with the demand for it. It was read everywhere apparently, and by everybody, and received with great acclamation. "Uncle Tom's Cabin" greatly influenced the Civil War which followed.

Mrs. Harriet Beecher Stowe was indeed the woman who "snapped the chains of slavery;" and it must have been a supreme joy to her that God permitted her to see the answer to her many prayers—the abolition of slavery. Her trust in God and love to Christ runs as a golden thread throughout her long life.

CHAPTER IX

Mary Slessor

MARY MITCHELL SLESSOR was born December 2nd, 1848, at Gilcomston, Scotland.   Her mother lovingly trained her children for time and for Eternity. She was "a wild lassie," but early in life she made the "great decision" for God "through the instrumentality of an old widow."

At eleven she began to earn her livelihood in a factory. As her mind opened she was eager for study, and would carry a book with her to the mill, lay it on the loom and glance at it in her free moments. So anxious was she to learn that she read on her way to and from the factory.

She was always interested in Foreign Missions. Years flew apace, and in May, 1875, Mary Slessor offered her services to the Foreign Mission Board.   Her heart was set on Calabar. She was accepted as a teacher for Calabar, and when her training was over, she sailed on August 5th, 1876, at the age of twenty-eight.

And in Calabar (Africa) Mary Slessor worked earnestly in the Lord's service for many years, sacrificing self for the good of others. She acquired a mastery of the language, so that she might enter into the life and thought of the natives. She was great at visiting among the people, coming in close touch with them. She found the climate of Calabar very trying—the rainy seasons, but especially the dry, because of the *harmattan*, a haze composed of fine dust blown from the African desert; it seemed to take all the energy out of her. She frequently had fever, but her faith never wavered.

She had great presence of mind. Once she noticed on the Cameron a tornado was coming on. She kept indoors sewing. The wind was furious, lifting fences, canoes, trees, and buildings; lightning and thunder

and rain poured down.   Then a column
of flame leapt from the sky to earth, and
a terrific crash.   The slaves rushed into the
yard, shrieking, and at that moment the
roof of her hut was swept away.   It was
appalling.   The flashes of lightning enabled
her to wade through the water, ankle deep,
and get wraps from her boxes.   To cheer
up the children, she started a hymn, and
gradually their terror ceased; but afterwards she was dangerously ill for two days.

In 1880 she was given work to accomplish in Old Town, an unworked province.
The people were amongst the most de-
graded in Calabar; it was a difficult field,
but Mary Slessor entered upon her new
labours with zest.   Here heathen iniquities
were practised—twin murder, human sacri-
fice, the stripping and flogging of women
by Egbo runners, and other offences.
Her sympathetic and affectionate personality gained for her great confidence and
love amongst the people.

Then came a time in Mary Slessor's life

when a sense of desolation and loneliness almost unsupportable swept over her. Her much-loved mother was "called Home," and Mary felt her loss keenly. She was benumbed. The sweet sympathy of home life was closed for ever. But she was not utterly alone, for she had her Lord's loving sympathy, and with characteristic "grit" she started forth again upon her life's work in "the strength of the Lord God."

Wonderful were her adventures, and marvellously was she rescued by the mighty hand of God from imminent danger. She was an intensely brave woman, fearless in the presence of the heathen chiefs, over whom she had great power. She was a loving student of the Bible, and a woman of prayer; but she could be as stern and strong as her native countrywomen when combating evil.

In her isolation and loneliness, she was only sustained by her faith in the efficacy of prayer. She was a woman who believed in prayer.

Gradually the work grew, she had break-downs, and then she would go back to her work again, eager and zealous as ever.

At one time Mary Slessor rendered important service to the Mission by her testimony before an Imperial Government Commission, which had been sent out to investigate the effect of the import, sale, and consumption of alcoholic liquor in Southern Nigeria. She provided convincing evidence of the demoralisation caused through drink.

Building, cementing, painting, varnishing, teaching and preaching filled in the days. A visitor found her once at 10 a.m., finishing school in a shed. She continued it in the afternoon. Then she visited the yards of the people, and they crowded round her, and brought her gifts of food. Later she leant against a fallen tree trunk and talked to one and another. In the gathering dusk she sat on a small stool and attended to the sick and dressed their sores. After dinner some men and lads arrived carrying lamps, and she held her catechumen's class, a very earnest and prayerful gathering.

Prayer enabled Mary Slessor to triumph over all obstacles, and her testimony to answered prayer was wonderful. She had a firm belief in God answering prayer; she knew He did; she had proved He did during all the years of her service for Him in the wilds of Africa.

She could indeed echo the words of the little hymn:

> "I believe God answers prayer,
> I am sure God answers prayer,
> I can prove God answers prayer.
> Glory to His Name!"

She was an earnest and intelligent student of the Bible, and to her it grew more wonderful every day; her Bible was well marked.

Mary Slessor received a Silver Cross for "meritorious services" from the Order of the Hospital of St. John of Jerusalem in England.

At last Mary Slessor's long life of self-less service was over, and she "passed away to be with Christ. " For many years, with brief and infrequent visits to England, Mary Slessor had laboured among the people of the Eastern Provinces in the South of Nigeria; thousands of natives loved and esteemed her, and her memory will live long in the hearts of her friends, native and European, in Nigeria.

Love for Christ made her a missionary and a heroine, love kept her toiling for those thirty-nine long years, and love was rewarded at last.

Chapter X

Elizabeth Fry

DURING a visit to London (when a girl) Elizabeth Gurney met an aged friend, Deborah Darby, who, on seeing the youthful, earnest girl, prophesied that she would be "A light to the blind, speech to the dumb, and feet to the lame." It made a great impression on her. In after years these words were in a striking manner fulfilled.

ELIZABETH GURNEY, one of ten children, was born in Norwich on May 21st, 1780. Her parents were Quakers—her father a banker, a broad-minded man of keen intellect; her mother was a highly cultured woman, whose loss Elizabeth felt keenly when young.

The preaching of William Savery at the yearly meeting was the means of arousing

Elizabeth, and she began to tire of her life of pleasure and seek after higher things. She laid aside music and dancing, and outward adornments, and adopted the rigid Quaker garments.

In 1800 she was married to Joseph Fry, a junior partner in the Bank. They resided in the house of business, St. Mildred's Court, London. Her life became very busy. Mr. and Mrs. Fry kept open house. Then as time sped on, the children came. There was a large household to keep up, visitors to entertain, constant correspondence with her sisters, and times of retirement never broken into. She was appointed by the Friends as visitor to the school and workhouse at Islington. Still she was not satisfied, she longed for a larger sphere of labour, for more personal contact with the poor.

After the death of her husband's father they removed to the old and beautiful family residence in Plashet, Essex. After the smoke and din of London, the beauties

of nature were a great joy to Mrs. Fry.
God was gently leading His child, as He
always does when His faithful ones are
longing to do His will.

In 1813 Elizabeth Fry paid her first
visit to Newgate (at the request of a friend),
in company with the sister of Sir
Fowell Buxton. The state of prisons at
this time was deplorable. All were herded
together, hardly any bedding was allowed,
no coals or candles; young and old, crimi-
nals, lunatics, debtors, and children.
The women were ferocious, and the atmos-
phere was fetid; the abandonment and
wickedness were indescribable. Drink was
sold to any who had money. The whole
system was one of bribery and corruption.
The jailers were often very little better,
morally, than the prisoners.

When they went they found three hundred women with their numerous children
crowded together, without classification or
employment of any kind, in the custody
of a man and his son. They cooked, they

washed, they slept on the floor. Elizabeth
Fry and her friend entered the cells
(repulsive though they were) and spoke to
them. Her loving heart was filled with the
deepest pity and sympathy for them, and
she longed to do something for their
permanent welfare.

The second time she went to Newgate
she begged to be left alone with the women,
and her request was granted. She read to
them, spoke to them of the Saviour's love,
and then appealed to them to help her in
some scheme for the education of the
children. She was touched with their
response and evident desire for the advantage of their children. Family events—
sickness and sorrow—prevented her from
visiting again for a considerable time,
and she could do little beyond sending
frequent gifts of clothing to the poor
prisoners.

In 1817 Mrs. Fry again took up the
threads of her life's work. The prisoners
hailed with tears of joy Mrs. Fry's proposal

MARY SLESSOR TRAVELLING DOWN THE RIVER IN A NATIVE
CANOE   (Chapter IX)

GRACE DARLING AND HER FATHER ROWING TO THE WRECK
OF THE "FORFARSHIRE" (Page 94)

to teach the children, and they chose from amongst themselves a suitable person for the post. She and her noble band of helpers devoted themselves to the work amid great discouragement from the City Magistrates. But the experiment was tried, and the result is expressed thus: "They saw no more an assemblage of abandoned and shameless creatures, half naked and half drunk, rather demanding than requesting charity. The prison no more resounded with obscenity and imprecations and licentious songs."

Between the years 1818 until her last illness in 1841, she visited, with one exception, every transport which sailed from England with women convicts bound for Botany Bay, trying to alleviate the condition of their surroundings.

In a report from the House of Commons, her work was spoken of in the highest terms of appreciation, and also in the House of Lords. Her work was arduous—her daughters helped her continually with her

6

correspondence—letters from all parts of the country about her Newgate work.

She went through a fiery ordeal and suffered deeply in her endeavours to suppress capital punishment for forgery.

Here is an example of her remarkable influence. A prisoner confessed years after when in Sydney of having resented Mrs. Fry's sermon (as she called it), trying to avoid listening by counting to herself. In taking leave of the prisoners, Mrs. Fry called this young woman aside and, putting her hand on her shoulder, said firmly and slowly: "Let not thine eyes covet." No other words passed her lips but these. "Her words were low and awful; kind as a mother, yet like a judge." When the young woman got to the colony she went on right enough for a time, but, one day she was looking into a box belonging to her mistress, and a gold thimble tempted her. It was on her finger in an instant; but just as she was shutting down the lid she felt Mrs. Fry's firm hand on her shoulder, the pleading touch of her fingers. She gave one look about her, threw back the thimble and trembled with terror to find she was alone in the room!

The secret of Mrs. Fry's power lay in her consciousness of the Divine Presence. "Thou hast been my stronghold, my Rock and my Fortress," she often wrote in her journal.

To reform the outward surroundings was Mrs. Fry's constant effort, but she never neglected to put before them God's claim: salvation through the death of the Lord Jesus Christ.

A friend who accompanied Mrs. Fry to Newgate, and was present when she read a portion of the Scriptures to the women, writes: "After a pause for silent prayer of some minutes, she quietly opened the volume and turned to the fifty-third chapter of Isaiah. The solemn reverence of her manner, the articulation so exquisitely modulated, so distinct, that not a word of that sweet and touching voice could fail to be heard. While she read, her mind seemed to be intensely absorbed in the passage of Scripture, and in nothing else. She set forth clearly and forcibly, though with a mild persuasiveness, the wonderful love of God. And wonderful were the testimonies from the women themselves, how they loved and reverenced her!

Notwithstanding the honour and respect in which she was held, she had genuine humility, and prayed for help and strength in that direction.

In 1825 and 1826 a great financial sorrow overtook the family, and they had to leave their home at Plashet. But the woman who had trusted God in prosperity and had *done* His will, now testified that she could trust God in adversity and *suffer* His will. Not only were these prison reforms carried on at Newgate, but they extended to many towns in England and to Ireland.

She keenly felt her children uniting themselves with other companies outside the Friends, but with sweet Christian charity, she said: "If, having sought to know the will of God as revealed in your hearts by His Spirit, and as taught in the Holy Scriptures, your conclusion is that you ought to join yourselves to any other Church than ours, I bid you God-speed in this."

Elizabeth Fry had a call to see her Majesty, the young Queen, who was to be married to Prince Albert; she found her interested and sympathetic. She travelled much in connection with her work.

Then came a time of weary suffering, but through all, her faith and trust never wavered; and then came the call for this devoted disciple and she "passed away to be with Christ."

Elizabeth Fry was one who lived daily near the Lord, and so was able to hear His voice, and she absolutely surrendered to His guidance.

CHAPTER XI

Charlotte Maria Tucker

NUMBER Three, Upper Portland Place, W., was the happy home of A.L.O.E. (A Lady of England) for nearly fifty years.

CHARLOTTE MARIA TUCKER was born at Frien Hatch, near Barnet, Middlesex, on May 8th, 1821. Her father was one of the Directors of the East India Company, whose life testified to his faith, and Charlotte spoke of her "sweet mother" whom all the children reverenced and loved. Charlotte was about fifteen, when (as she said) "the feeling of being His and indeed having the Saviour as *my own* Saviour came upon me like a flood of daylight, I was so happy."

The years of her home life, although simple and quiet, were bright with acts of loving service. A sorrow fell across "Number Three" when the honoured and loved father was called Home.

About this time Charlotte first published her stories for children. "The Claremont Tales." In writing to a publisher, she says: "I ask for no earthly remuneration, my position in life renders me independent of any exertions of my own. I pray but for God's blessing upon my attempts to instruct His lambs in the things which concern their everlasting welfare."

She desired to yield her pen to the service of her Heavenly Father, and in all her writings sought that His Name might be honoured; and she had marked success.

Charlotte Tucker did not write for a livelihood, she had an income of her own, and she is believed to have devoted most, or all, of the proceeds of her pen to charitable purposes. All her many books have a definite purpose in them—a high moral tone—their object to teach and help

Heavenward all their readers. She had a wonderful vitality and mental vigour. She rose early and secured at least an hour's writing before breakfast.

In 1869 she was called upon to part from her "sweetest mother," to whom she had always yielded implicit obedience, love, and reverence. Then the old home, "Number Three," was broken up. After this followed a few years of usefulness, working for the Master whom she loved and honoured, and then closed the quiet years of home life, and Charlotte Maria Tucker was called to public service abroad.

At the age of *fifty-four*, in the year 1875, Miss Tucker definitely settled to go out as a Missionary to India at her own expense. Brave, selfless woman! The Indian climate did not impair her health, she had a wonderful constitution, although the weather was very changeable; burning heat, bitter cold, or furious rains; all three in the course of a week.

There are lights and shadows in mis-

sionary life. Amidst all her disappoint-
ments her trust never failed. Her heart's
desire was to live and toil in Batala, yet
a deeper desire was to carry out His will.
As a rule the afternoons were filled up by
her with study of the language, reading,
writing, etc.

Zenana visiting was only one portion of
her work. She was a warm and true friend
to the Indian Christians, entered into their
trials and difficulties; doing her utmost to
help them upward and onward.   She was
deeply attached to the people—called them
her *brown friends*. A school of Panjabi
boys was removed from Amritsar to the
Old Palace at Batala, under the presidency
of the Rev. Francis Baring. Miss Tucker
was a great blessing among the Christian
boys at the school; she had a wonderful
influence over them and loved them.
Here she lived on year after year. The
merry boys in the school were very dear
to her.

In the years 1884 and 1885 Miss

Tucker's loneliest time in Batala was over. She now lived with the family of the Principal of the school, and two other lady missionaries settled in Batala to help on the work.

It does indeed need God-given courage to confess Christ in India. The true hearted ones make the plunge at last. "The love of Christ constraineth. "

She wrote stories for the people and had them printed in the language at her own expense.

The last eighteen years of her life were the fullest and busiest. At an advanced age she could accomplish much: vast correspondence, reading, literary composition, school classes, Bible meetings, and various interviews; hers was indeed a full life of loving service for the Master.

CHAPTER XII

Grace Darling

GRACE HORSLEY DARLING was
born at Bamborough, in Northumberland, on Nov. 24th, 1817. Her
father, William Darling, was keeper of
the Longstone Lighthouse, on the Farne
Islands. Her parents were Christians.

Northumberland's heroine, Grace, is
associated with the Harear Rocks, on
which the "Forfarshire" struck at three
o'clock on a wild tempestuous September
morning in 1838. She was bound from
Hull to Dundee with sixty-three persons
on board, forty-three were drowned. The
stern, quarter deck, and cabins were swept
down the furious channel, called the Piper
Gut, while the other half of the vessel
remained on the rock. Such of the pas-
sengers who survived clung to the swaying

vessel as the waves dashed over it, threatening death at every crash.

The sky was black, the sea swollen. The old leak broke out again. "How will they keep the engine fires alight? The weather's full of mischief. There is fog as well as gale ahead of us," an old sailor said. The dark clouds looked bulging down on the "Forfarshire." Darkness fell swiftly. The wind rose to a whining shriek. The vessel went haltingly on her way.

Presently there was a rush of feet and the shouting of new orders. "We must hoist the sails, the fires are out!" The ship was being driven southward. The heavy seas which lifted her up and dashed her down again could hardly be seen for a fog and rain. Suddenly out of the dusk ahead towered a black mass. A violent shock ran through the vessel. Human voices screamed: "She has struck. We are wrecked."

A terrible scene followed, people running

to and fro, wailing for help, which no one could give; the waves pounded her like sledge hammers and then rushed roaring over the decks, sweeping them clean of everything. All at once a greater wave lifted its head from the sea, hovered a moment, and then fell.

The ship was lifted, but immediately fell down again. There was a noise of tearing and crashing like the fall of a forest. She broke in half, and the hind part was swept away by the current, the fore part was wedged on the rock.

The seas thundered to and fro. The morning grew grey on a scene of unabated storm. Daylight found nine people waiting for the end. Across the sea, on one of the black rock islands, a tall finger pointed to the sky. It was the Longstone Lighthouse.

Grace Darling and her father, William Darling, heard the cries and screams of human voices from the lighthouse, and they determined to reach the wreck, and if possible rescue the only survivors clinging

to the rocks, at all costs. They recognised
that though they might be able to get to
the wreck, they would be unable to return
without the assistance of the shipwrecked
crew; but, nothing daunted, they took this
risk without hesitation. By a combination
of daring, strength, and skill, and with a
courage which faced difficulties, without
thinking of self, father and daughter set
off.

A boy on the wreck was eagerly watch-
ing a black speck riding on the waves by
the lighthouse, and he screamed: "It's a
boat!" Someone said: "No boat could
live in such a sea." But presently faint
voices were clamouring with him. "It *is*
a boat." Up and down the waves danced,
drawing steadily nearer.

There were two people in it. The boat
came on, and reached some low lying
rocks near by. One of the people got out
and began to creep towards the wreck,
while the other held the boat. One by one
the rescuers had to lead the survivors

over the rocks to the boat. The boy's turn came last. "Is there none below?" asked the lighthouseman, William Darling. He and the boy climbed down.

In the forecabin they found a woman clasping two children in her arms. They were dead. Gently the lighthouseman discovered that the woman still lived; and alone, for the boy was too weak to help, he bore her up to the ruined deck. "A little longer," he said, "and you'd have been like these poor children. When I saw the wreck this morning, I didn't dream there could be anyone on her; but my daughter, Grace, said she could see people through the glass. Then I didn't believe we could reach you, but she would have us try, and we came with her mother's blessing."

The opportunity came to her, and she responded without hesitation, utterly ignoring self. This gallant exploit made Grace Darling and her father famous. The Humane Society at once voted them its gold medal, the Treasury made a grant, and a public subscription was organised. The exposure was great, and this brave young girl, who had always been delicate, died of consumption on October 20th, 1842, four years after the rescue.

There is a fine Norman Church at Bamborough, in Northumberland, and in the north transcept there is a figure—the Northumberland heroine, Grace Darling, resting with an oar by her side. Her name lives for evermore here, where the sea boils around the rocks that witnessed her daring, and in all lands where the English tongue is spoken.